THE *longing of* GOD'S *heart* IS FOR US *to know him*

Prayer Journal

ISBN - 9781670515803
978-1-7336203-5-2

Date ____________________

Scriptures I read today

Prayer Requests

I am grateful for

Daily Prayer

Father,

Amen

Date God moved on my behalf

____

Miracles, dreams and God encounters I experienced today,

Healing Exodus 15:26, 23:25

If you listen carefully to the voice of the Lord your God & do what is right in his eyes, if you pay attention to his commands & keep all his decrees, I will not bring on any of the diseases I brought on the Egyptians, for I am the Lord who heals you.

Deuteronomy 7:4-15 30:19-20

John 3:17

(1) God never condemns you!

Don't shame people or condemn them

Jesus never did this!

(2) If you have blown it — Confess it!

Tell God and ask to move forward

(3) Accept God's mercy & his love.

It's new every morning

forgiveness is already!

(4) Realize that God is still working on you!

Speak against that condemnation!

His grace is sufficient!

Do not receive it!

It's a confidence stopper!

Confidence brings the reward

No shame

No fear

All confidence!

My Concerns I gave to God today

Love

Well today!

Date ____________________

Scriptures I read today

Prayer Requests

I am grateful for

Daily Prayer

Father,

Amen

Date God moved on my behalf

Miracles, dreams and God encounters I experienced today,

My Concerns I gave to God today

Love

Never fails!

Date ____________________

Scriptures I read today

Prayer Requests

I am grateful for

Daily Prayer

Father,

Amen

Date God moved on my behalf

Miracles, dreams and God encounters I experienced today,

I will make your journey

with ME worth it

My Concerns I gave to God today

Hope

In all things!

Date ____________________

Scriptures I read today

Prayer Requests

I am grateful for

Daily Prayer

Father,

Amen

Date God moved on my behalf

____

Miracles, dreams and God encounters I experienced today,

My Concerns I gave to God today

Be a carrier of

Peace

Date ____________________

Scriptures I read today

Prayer Requests

I am grateful for

Daily Prayer

Father,

Amen

Date God moved on my behalf

Miracles, dreams and God encounters I experienced today,

My Concerns I gave to God today

Honor God with your

Choices!

Date ____________________

Scriptures I read today

Prayer Requests

I am grateful for

Daily Prayer

Father,

Amen

Date God moved on my behalf

____

Miracles, dreams and God encounters I experienced today,

My Concerns I gave to God today

There is

Power

In the Blood

Date ____________________

Scriptures I read today

Prayer Requests

I am grateful for

Daily Prayer

Father,

Amen

Date God moved on my behalf

____

Miracles, dreams and God encounters I experienced today,

My Concerns I gave to God today

Guard your

Thoughts

Date ____________________

Scriptures I read today

Prayer Requests

I am grateful for

Daily Prayer

Father,

Amen

Date God moved on my behalf

____

Miracles, dreams and God encounters I experienced today,

My Concerns I gave to God today

Leave a legacy of

Love

Date ____________________

Scriptures I read today

Prayer Requests

I am grateful for

Daily Prayer

Father,

Amen

Date God moved on my behalf

Miracles, dreams and God encounters I experienced today,

My Concerns I gave to God today

Always Be

Kind

Date ____________________

Scriptures I read today

Prayer Requests

I am grateful for

Daily Prayer

Father,

Amen

Date God moved on my behalf

____

Miracles, dreams and God encounters I experienced today,

My Concerns I gave to God today

Be found

Faithful

Date ____________________

Scriptures I read today

Prayer Requests

I am grateful for

Daily Prayer

Father,

Amen

Date God moved on my behalf

____

Miracles, dreams and God encounters I experienced today,

My Concerns I gave to God today

Share your

Light

with others

Date ____________________

Scriptures I read today

Prayer Requests

I am grateful for

Daily Prayer

Father,

Amen

Date God moved on my behalf

Miracles, dreams and God encounters I experienced today,

My Concerns I gave to God today

Have

Faith

In God

Date ____________________

Scriptures I read today

Prayer Requests

I am grateful for

Daily Prayer

Father,

Amen

Date God moved on my behalf

Miracles, dreams and God encounters I experienced today,

My Concerns I gave to God today

Joy

Comes In the morning

Date ____________________

Scriptures I read today

Prayer Requests

I am grateful for

Daily Prayer

Father,

Amen

Date God moved on my behalf

Miracles, dreams and God encounters I experienced today,

My Concerns I gave to God today

Your *Praise*

moves mountains!

Date ____________________

Scriptures I read today

Prayer Requests

I am grateful for

Daily Prayer

Father,

Amen

Date God moved on my behalf

____

Miracles, dreams and God encounters I experienced today,

My Concerns I gave to God today

There is power in your

Prayers

Date ____________________

Scriptures I read today

Prayer Requests

I am grateful for

Daily Prayer

Father,

Amen

Date God moved on my behalf

Miracles, dreams and God encounters I experienced today,

My Concerns I gave to God today

Always be

Grateful

Date ____________________

Scriptures I read today

Prayer Requests

I am grateful for

Daily Prayer

Father,

Amen

Date God moved on my behalf

Miracles, dreams and God encounters I experienced today,

My Concerns I gave to God today

Share your

Hope

with others!

Date ____________________

Scriptures I read today

Prayer Requests

I am grateful for

Daily Prayer

Father,

Amen

Date God moved on my behalf

____

Miracles, dreams and God encounters I experienced today,

My Concerns I gave to God today

Think about

Others

Date ____________________

Scriptures I read today

Prayer Requests

I am grateful for

Daily Prayer

Father,

Amen

Date God moved on my behalf

____

Miracles, dreams and God encounters I experienced today,

My Concerns I gave to God today

Share your

Smile

Date ____________________

Scriptures I read today

Prayer Requests

I am grateful for

Daily Prayer

Father,

Amen

Date God moved on my behalf

____

Miracles, dreams and God encounters I experienced today,

My Concerns I gave to God today

Give others

Grace

Date ___________________

Scriptures I read today

Prayer Requests

I am grateful for

Daily Prayer

Father,

Amen

Date God moved on my behalf

____

Miracles, dreams and God encounters I experienced today,

My Concerns I gave to God today

Forgive

and let go!

Date ____________________

Scriptures I read today

Prayer Requests

I am grateful for

Daily Prayer

Father,

Amen

Date God moved on my behalf

Miracles, dreams and God encounters I experienced today,

My Concerns I gave to God today

Encourage others

with your

Words

Date ___________________

Scriptures I read today

Prayer Requests

I am grateful for

Daily Prayer

Father,

Amen

My Concerns I gave to God today

Cultivate a

Heart

of giving!

Date ____________________

Scriptures I read today

Prayer Requests

I am grateful for

Daily Prayer

Father,

Amen

Date God moved on my behalf

____

Miracles, dreams and God encounters I experienced today,

My Concerns I gave to God today

Stay

humble

Date ____________________

Scriptures I read today

Prayer Requests

I am grateful for

Daily Prayer

Father,

Amen

Date God moved on my behalf

____

Miracles, dreams and God encounters I experienced today,

My Concerns I gave to God today

Be

thoughtful

Date ____________________

Scriptures I read today

Prayer Requests

I am grateful for

Daily Prayer

Father,

Amen

Date God moved on my behalf

____

Miracles, dreams and God encounters I experienced today,

My Concerns I gave to God today

Be a carrier of

God's

Presence

Date ____________________

Scriptures I read today

Prayer Requests

I am grateful for

Daily Prayer

Father,

Amen

Date God moved on my behalf

____

Miracles, dreams and God encounters I experienced today,

My Concerns I gave to God today

Inspire

others!

Date ____________________

Scriptures I read today

Prayer Requests

I am grateful for

Daily Prayer

Father,

Amen

Date God moved on my behalf

____

Miracles, dreams and God encounters I experienced today,

My Concerns I gave to God today

Be

Hopeful

Date ____________________

Scriptures I read today

Prayer Requests

I am grateful for

Daily Prayer

Father,

Amen

Date God moved on my behalf

Miracles, dreams and God encounters I experienced today,

My Concerns I gave to God today

Storms

are meant to make you stronger!

Date ____________________

Scriptures I read today

Prayer Requests

I am grateful for

Daily Prayer

Father,

Amen

Date God moved on my behalf

Miracles, dreams and God encounters I experienced today,

My Concerns I gave to God today

Enjoy every

Moment

Date ____________________

Scriptures I read today

Prayer Requests

I am grateful for

Daily Prayer

Father,

Amen

Date God moved on my behalf

____

Miracles, dreams and God encounters I experienced today,

My Concerns I gave to God today

Be

Thankful

for everything!

Date ____________________

Scriptures I read today

Prayer Requests

I am grateful for

Daily Prayer

Father,

Amen

Date God moved on my behalf

Miracles, dreams and God encounters I experienced today,

My Concerns I gave to God today

Guard your

Heart

Date ____________________

Scriptures I read today

Prayer Requests

I am grateful for

Daily Prayer

Father,

Amen

Date God moved on my behalf

____

Miracles, dreams and God encounters I experienced today,

My Concerns I gave to God today

Grow

Goodness

Date ____________________

Scriptures I read today

Prayer Requests

I am grateful for

Daily Prayer

Father,

Amen

Date God moved on my behalf

Miracles, dreams and God encounters I experienced today,

My Concerns I gave to God today

Plant seeds of

Love

Date ____________________

Scriptures I read today

Prayer Requests

I am grateful for

Daily Prayer

Father,

Amen

Date God moved on my behalf

Miracles, dreams and God encounters I experienced today,

My Concerns I gave to God today

Be

Teachable

Date ____________________

Scriptures I read today

Prayer Requests

I am grateful for

Daily Prayer

Father,

Amen

Date God moved on my behalf

Miracles, dreams and God encounters I experienced today,

My Concerns I gave to God today

Trust

In God

Date ___________________

Scriptures I read today

Prayer Requests

I am grateful for

Daily Prayer

Father,

Amen

Date God moved on my behalf

Miracles, dreams and God encounters I experienced today,

My Concerns I gave to God today

There is power in your

Words

Date ____________________

Scriptures I read today

Prayer Requests

I am grateful for

Daily Prayer

Father,

Amen

Date God moved on my behalf

____

Miracles, dreams and God encounters I experienced today,

My Concerns I gave to God today

Live with

Passion

Date ___________________

Scriptures I read today

Prayer Requests

I am grateful for

Daily Prayer

Father,

Amen

Date God moved on my behalf

Miracles, dreams and God encounters I experienced today,

My Concerns I gave to God today

Be

Excellent

in all you do!

Date ____________________

Scriptures I read today

Prayer Requests

I am grateful for

Daily Prayer

Father,

Amen

Date God moved on my behalf

Miracles, dreams and God encounters I experienced today,

My Concerns I gave to God today

Live without

Regrets

Date ____________________

Scriptures I read today

Prayer Requests

I am grateful for

Daily Prayer

Father,

Amen

Date God moved on my behalf

Miracles, dreams and God encounters I experienced today,

My Concerns I gave to God today

Respond well to

God's Voice

Date ____________________

Scriptures I read today

Prayer Requests

I am grateful for

Daily Prayer

Father,

Amen

Date God moved on my behalf

Miracles, dreams and God encounters I experienced today,

My Concerns I gave to God today

Live life with

Heaven-filled purpose

Date ____________________

Scriptures I read today

Prayer Requests

I am grateful for

Daily Prayer

Father,

Amen

Date God moved on my behalf

Miracles, dreams and God encounters I experienced today,

My Concerns I gave to God today

Sing to the

Lord

a new song

Review

Made in USA - North Chelmsford, MA
1039366_9781670515803
12.23.2019 1055